WHY WOMEN ARE
SO EMOTIONALLY
ATTACHED
AND MEN ARE NOT?

WHY WOMEN ARE SO EMOTIONALLY ATTACHED AND MEN ARE NOT?

V. CLERVE MSN

To order additional copies of this book, contact:
Xlibris Corporation
1-888-795-4274
www.Xlibris.com
Orders@Xlibris.com
40771

DEDICATION

To the men and women who display their genuine emotions toward one another, to the women who have opened my eyes about emotion, and to all my friends at the hospital and abroad.

Introduction

THE BELIEF THAT women are *emotionally attached* and men are not is an everyday conversation between friends and families. As a nurse, I trained to provide care to patients and families, thus becoming a patient's advocate. I trained to be an empathizer and to be unemotionally attached to patients. The question I pose every day is why men are not emotionally attached as women are. In many instances, my colleagues at work show their emotions in emergent situations, and I applaud them for that. However, I still wonder why men are not emotionally attached as women are. My aim in this book is to answer such question after having researched some probable causes. Perhaps the easiest way for people to convey their emotions and connect with each other is by sharing the stories of their life and their personal opinions.

ANECDOTAL VIEWS

THE *WEBSTER* DICTIONARY defines emotions as the sentimental aspect of feelings. In addition, it defines feelings as a personal reaction to a person, place, or thing. When we heed or notice something with emotional basis, we retort to what we feel. Despite the situations, we cannot keep emotions away from our lives. Some genders are good in keeping them from coming out and some aren't.

CHAPTER 1

WHY DO EMOTIONS have real impacts in our lives? This is a question that could be answered with various feasibilities corresponding to one another. Perhaps emotions have a single fundamental meaning or code—that of producing a retort in people and their upbringing; or perhaps emotions have real impacts in our lives in order to be our primary funnel of communication; or they may precisely have real impacts in order to regulate our self-belief.

CHAPTER 2

MANY CULTURES ARROGATE a great dissimilarity in the way men and women experience emotions. Women are simulated to be more emotionally attached than men, both experiencing inner emotions, as well as expressing them to others. While the genders may disagree in how they utter or share their emotions, men and women naturally differed from one another when expressing their emotions. Research suggests that men and women experience a noticeable dissimilarity in ways they express their emotions. Many times, men tend to show their emotion with their mind. In contrast, women show their emotion with their heart.

Women are thought to experience more frequent and more passionate emotions, whereas men are thought to be emotionless and to have less passionate touching experience. Many have analyzed whether gender-emotion differs according to the situation or environment. After analyzing this subject, it is very difficult to say whether emotions are connected with the female or male pigeonhole. Specifically, our society is prone to connect cheerfulness, grief, and apprehension with women, whereas they tend to tie aggression with men.

I believe that emotions vary between men and women. Both men and women may experience joy in a parallel way, but women are inclined to express their emotions of happiness regardless of the situation, whereas men tend to manage them. When women express their emotions, some men see that as being insecure. However, when men do not show their emotions, some women see that as being impassive.

CHAPTER 3

TO SPECIFICALLY ANSWER this question about why women are emotionally attached and men are not, I interviewed some men and women regarding this genuine topic. Here are some examples of their views:

Jesse: My view on that issue is that there is a chromosomal defect in men. Men are born handicapped at birth because one arm of the X chromosome has been broken.

Jhoanna: I do not believe in Jesse's view. I think the brain of women and men are different and that we are brought up differently.

Debra: As for me, I believe that there is a hormonal difference. That is to say, we have different chemistry.

Adrienne: I do not agree that men are not emotionally attached. Men may not show outwardly their feelings, but I believe they are emotionally attached to the people they love. I also have observed how attached they are to their pets, especially their dogs. However, said Adrienne, women need relationships to survive and nurture one another. I believe this all stems from early days when women maintained the hearth, and men were the hunters and protectors.

Bella: It is a woman's nature to be emotional.

Sandy: My experience has been that there are men as well as women who are emotionally attached either to people or objects. I believe it depends on one's personal makeup combined with one's upbringing and nurturing. It seems most people base an attachment on experience, positive reinforcement, and sense of self.

Andrea: I think men have the desire to be emotional, but they do not know how to express it.

Bob: Women are like roses, and men are like the thorns. Men do not flourish like women do. By expressing different views regarding emotions between these two genders, men tend to be more reserved than women. Women are like the roots of roses, they are always alive and ready to give emotional food in order to nurture men.

Cristina: When my boyfriend broke up with me, I was devastated that he did not drop one tear from his eyes and thus thought that he never loved me. How could he not cry if the woman that he supposedly loved so much was no longer going to be in his life? For sure, I thought he really never had any emotions.

Marian: It goes back to women being the nesters and men being the hunters. Women spend time at the nest, and men have to be ready to move the tribe to a better, new home.

How do emotions start? Listen to a two-people conversation:

Joyce: Hi, John! This is Joyce.

John: I am glad you called! I missed talking to you.

Joyce: Me too, John.

John: I feel that we are not in the same page when we talk about emotions and feelings, Joyce.

Joyce: What do you mean, John?

John: I felt disrespected by you last week after calling me so many names.

Joyce: I am really sorry, John. I have made a terrible mistake, one that deserves no forgiveness. I should think before saying something. I should control my emotions. Despite that, I am asking you to please forgive me. I am fully committed for that to never happen again.

John: You really hurt me when you said these things to me, Joyce.

Joyce: I was really hurting when you said I was insecure, John. That is the reason why I said many bad things to you.

John: The reason why I said that you were insecure was because you said that you don't know if I have any emotions for you. I told you over and over again, Joyce, that you are in my heart day and night. Moreover, you want me to marry you after seeing each other for four weeks, Joyce.

Joyce: I am a woman, John, and I am at age. I need to know where I stand with you. Truly, John, I really love you and only want to love you and respect you and honor you and take care of you. This is the truth. I miss you incredibly, and I really wish that you would give me one last, and I mean the very last, chance; and let me prove in action these words I am saying to you.

John: It's getting late, Joyce. I'll talk to you soon. I will think about everything you just said. Good night.

Joyce: Do we have any hope together?

John: Good night, Joyce

Joyce: Okay! Good night.

Another Story of Emotions

This a phone conversation between a man and a woman.

Dowdy: Hello! Is Jimmie there?

Jimmie: This is he. How can I help you?

Dowdy: Hi, Jimmie! This is Dowdy. Can we talk about what happened the other day?

Jimmie: I am very busy right now. That's okay. I can give you few minutes.

Dowdy: Since we made love, Jimmie, you've been avoiding me. Did I do something wrong?

Jimmie: You did not do anything wrong, Dowdy. I just felt that we moved too quickly in that relationship.

Dowdy: What do you mean by moving too quickly?

Jimmie: We need to start seeing other people, Dowdy.

Dowdy: Why, Jimmie? Am I not the woman that you want?

Jimmie: I never said that. The only thing I am saying is that we need to start seeing other people.

Dowdy: You are the only person I want to have in my life, Jimmie. You are more than gold to me, Jimmie. You are the precious gift that I've been waiting for a long time.

Jimmie: You are too emotional for me, and I want to start exploring other people.

Dowdy: Why are you doing this to me, Jimmie? I thought we had something going on together. We slept together, we went out together. Now you are playing with my emotions.

Jimmie: You see what I said. I just said that you are too emotional.

Dowdy: I am a woman, Jimmie. Women have emotions. Women are emotional creatures. Truly, Jimmie, I am not a tree without emotions. Do you say that our relationship is over?

Jimmie: That's what I've been trying to tell you.

Dowdy: This is very painful, Jimmie. I keep thinking at the great and lost moments I have had with you: the nights you prepared meals for me, the time you will give me back massage and whisper in my ears loving words, the conversations we had outdoor, the dinners you took me out to, the time you picked me up in your arms and gracefully laid me on your couch. Truly, that was the most romantic time I have ever had in my life! The time we were daydreaming about the financial future as you were ironing, the time you were driving and talking business as a good steward, the time we sat across from each other at Starbucks sipping tea and having a good conversation. The times we were just able to sit on the couch in each other's presence. The times we flossed our teeth in front of each other. The time you would open the doors, to your home, to your cars. The time you have praised me and made me feel so beautiful and special like saying, "You are an amazing woman." The dreams I shared with you to become your wife someday and be the mother of your children. The time you said to me, "Hey, the house misses you." The times I got up to make us breakfast and to decorate the table for us. The time I was crying on your shoulder, and you gave me your handkerchief, and making the time to stay there and listen to me though you needed to go to work. And the time you drove to my house and picked me up to take me to a very fancy restaurant, and many more times than I could think of right now. Truly, Jimmie, you have treated me like a princess and know that the texting, the calling you over and over, the chasing after you, Jimmie. Do we have to throw all these away, Jimmie? I do not want to see other people, Jimmie. I only want you in my life. You know how I feel emotionally about you, Jimmie. Please let's stay together and enjoy life. That's all I want to say to you, Jimmie.

Jimmie: Thank you, Dowdy, for saying all these things. I will give you another chance, but we need to start working on our emotions.

Dowdy: Can I come to see you tomorrow, Jimmie?

Jimmie: You can come to see me. Bye!

Dowdy: See you tomorrow. Bye.

Marcus's Nightmare about Emotions

My friend Marcus went to visit his girlfriend one day around seven-thirty. When he got there, his girlfriend asked him what he wanted to do today. Marcus replied that he would like to take her out to a romantic dinner. She agreed to that idea. While waiting to be seated at the restaurant, Marcus stood up in one corner with his girlfriend beside him. Finally, a table for two was called. Luckily, it was Marcus and his girlfriend's table. They were sitting at the table, looking at each other, exchanging a romantic idea.

Suddenly, Marcus stayed quiet; then his girlfriend said, *"Marcus, what are you thinking?"* He said, *"I was just thinking what I wanted to get you for your birthday."*

The waitress brought the food for both, and they were eaten. At the end of dinner, Marcus drove his girlfriend back home.

When they arrived home, the girlfriend said, *"Marcus, I did not believe that you were thinking about what you wanted to buy me for my birthday. I think you were watching the girl sitting to the next table across us, and you did not pay attention to me,"*

Marcus said, *"Why would I want to look at the girl who was sitting across us?"*

Later, Marcus said, *"I do not understand you, Lisa. You need to control your emotional jealousy."*

For Marcus, this is a nightmare. According to him, his girlfriend is jealous and emotional. This story is very typical. Many times, women asked men questions that go like this: *"What are you thinking?"* I talked to many women about that question. This is what they said, *"Women asked that particular question because they are seeking for attention when they are with men."* They need to be reassured that they are in good hands and that they are secure. In contrast, men view this type of question as nightmares and burden.

CHAPTER 4

The Beauty of Emotions

NOT TOO LONG ago, I was invited to a birthday dinner party. While sitting on the table with three women, I could not stop listening to the conversation they were having. One of the women (Josephine) said, *"My husband understands very well my emotional needs because I trained him."* The other woman sitting next to her said, *"What do you mean?"* Josephine replied and said, *"When my husband got home from work, he fulfills my emotional needs. I know he is very tired because he works forty-five to fifty hours a week. However, he knows when I need to be cuddled.* She also said, *"When my husband went for a business trip, I wore his shirt or anything that had his smell."*

After listening to Josephine's story, I realized that she's trying to meet her emotional needs, and she feels happy and beautiful inside when that need is met. Emotions are as beautiful as a cool breeze in a summertime, beautiful as a bride who's waiting for her groom, as a mother who gives birth for the first time to her child.

Are women really emotionally attached, and men are not? The story of a woman's emotion.

Women are simulated to be more emotionally attached than men, but all human beings are full of emotions. Both men and women have similar types of emotions, but they are uttered in dissimilar behavior. When my sister's (Chrismene) ex-boyfriend broke up with her, she wanted to kill herself. She did not eat or drink. She kept wondering what she had done wrong to make him leave her. She cried every day. It was a very painful moment for her. When I asked why she felt this way, she replied, *"You would not understand a woman's emotion."* It was years later when I began to understand the dissimilarity between men's and women's emotions. Women's emotions consist of warmth, empathy, desires, affection, love, and attachments. Women display their emotions like a burning fire that keep others warm in a cold winter night. In contrast, men display their emotions like a fallen snow in a cold winter night where there is no passion, and no warmth.

Many psychologists and researchers note that men feel the emotion *"many times"* stronger than women do in spite of the surroundings. I tend to agree with that concept. However, men tend to hold their emotions within because of their upbringings and their surroundings. I remember when I used to cry as a boy, my dad used to tell me *"boys don't cry,"* and boys need *"to be tough."* In contrast, when my sister cried, my dad cuddled her and gave her a kiss. Because of that, I learned to hold my emotions in spite of the situations.

Human's environment plays a key aspect on how he or she expresses his or her emotions. Women tend to be more animated and less devious about their emotions, whereas men tend to hold them. Today, society and culture turn out to be the principal reason on how emotions have been viewed. For instance, a man who shows his emotions may be viewed as being *"weak."* Men are anticipated to be tough. In contrast, women are labeled to be subtle. Men's duties are to provide, care, and protect his family.

A Family's Story on Emotions

When I was growing up, I did not know what emotions really were. I witnessed many things that happened in my family. I witnessed a husband who did not know how to handle his wife's emotions, and a mother who reviled her daughter because she dishonored a family tradition. We were a family of five, but life was rosy and beautiful.

Friends praised us for the way we handled ourselves as a family. We could afford anything, but we were emotionally bankrupt.

I vividly remember when my mother threatened to leave my father because of lack of his emotional support. My father was a very successful man. He strongly believed in providing and taking care of his family. However, he failed to support his wife emotionally. It was a nightmare for my mother. The family became disharmonized. My sister married a man who kept abusing her emotionally, and my brother's wife passed away after giving birth to her first child. All these things ravaged the family nucleus, and friends started coming to our house to give advice and to provide support.

After remembering all these, one question I want to pose is, how strong are emotions? Emotions are stronger than adhesive that fastens a broken vase together. Not too long ago, my sister and her husband were arguing. After she called me and my brother to explain the situation, we decided to go to her house to pick her up in order to take her back to the family house. When we arrived to her house, she and her husband were still arguing. We asked her to go back home with us. She finally decided that she would leave. On our way out, her husband kept saying horrible things to her. My brother who was there with me could not stand those words said by my sister's husband. Therefore, he wanted to hit him, and I tried to stop my brother from doing so, but I was unsuccessful. When my sister realized that my brother could not stop, she cried and said, *"This is my husband, please do not hurt him. I love him very much, and I need him in my life."* My sister is one among many women facing emotional abuse. Because women are emotionally attached and men are not, women tend to suffer despite the level of the relationships.

Kathy's conversation regarding her emotion. The conversation goes like this:

"Kathy, tell me about your emotion for your boyfriend."

"I believe that showing my emotions openly to my boyfriend is very healthy," she replied.

Kathy does not hide her emotions when she argues with her boyfriend. She feels the need to say what's in her mind. However, her boyfriend tends to hide his emotion for her. There is a lesson to learn in Kathy's story. Men are conditioned to be strong, to show no weakness, to shed no tears; and women are the sensitive, emotional ones. I know many men who feel insulted if they are referred to as being too emotional.

I remember when my late girlfriend passed away many years ago; I had to give an acclamation at her funeral. I was very hesitant about that because I did not know how to express myself. My sister asked me to say something that I did with my girlfriend when she was alive. I recalled many stories, but the one that touched me the most was when my girlfriend used to call me every night before I go to bed just to say, *"I love you, honey, and always remember you are my emotional bank."* While I was telling the audience at the funeral what my girlfriend used to do, I started crying. It was a very painful time, and I needed to cry to release my emotions. It was then that I kept saying to myself that men need to let loose their emotion and stop holding them. Men need to realize that it is very healthy to display their emotions in private or in public.

CHAPTER 5

What Does Culture Have to Do with Emotion?

CULTURE PLAYS AN essential function in our world. We are an insecure species, and culture offers us standard rules of emotions. Culture offers certainty in an erratic world. Culture is a framework of mind that we urbanized during our upbringing. The structural worthiness, unity, and strength of our personalities are rooted in our culture. It is for these reasons that cultural relations can cause apprehension and stimulate emotions. Culture influences thoughts, emotions, and behaviors.

How Can One Explain Emotion?

One individual puts it this way: "Emotion is something that is unexplainable." It is true that both men and women may know what emotions are, but why do emotions happen, and why they generate mystification? The makeup of men and women is very convoluted. When something happens to us, we act according to our emotions. Emotions, as a whole, are very multifaceted. That is why they are bewildering and unexplainable.

Example of Emotional Reaction

When we see others being abused, we automatically feel pity or angry. When we see a sick person, we express our empathy. When an intimate relationship goes bad, we feel down and secluded. We experience feelings of great joy and happiness when we find bona fide love, give birth to a child, and fulfill our dreams. Being emotional is endless because we express our emotions with words that no one can validate except us. We may not know why, but we feel relieved after expressing them to others.

Why we experience these emotions, no one knows. All science does know are the "chemical reactions" that contribute to our emotions. It is hard to discern emotions from one person to another because each individual is very singular. We truly cannot say that a certain emotion is a certain obsession because there are no vocabularies that can be assumed as to how someone feels.

I suppose from the day that men and women are born, they start displaying their emotions toward certain things.

Even though men and women have emotions, they still have to discover what they are. There is no instruction manual that comes with men and women in order to tell them what to feel or when to feel something. Everyone has different views on what he or she is feeling. We may know what emotions are from learning they may be expressed differently to each person. For example, one person who feels happy may quiver all over, or someone may be filled with endless rage that leads to destruction.

If something happened in a community, the people would come together in order to support one another. This would be a social emotion that gives the sense of harmony and camaraderie.

There could be many ways to explain emotions, but the question will remain why women are emotionally attached and men are not. We may not have a definitive answer for that question. Perhaps we are not supposed to know why we have these emotions.

The secret why women are so emotionally attached and men are not is because men tend to hang on to the *"trivial acts"* of affection, and women tend to value them more. I remember when my ex-girlfriend used to hold me and kiss me in public. I felt embarrassed by it. She used to pet me. When I asked why she's doing all these, she said it is because she's an affectionate and emotional woman. It was weeks later when we broke up that I realized how emotionally attached she was. If I understood better her emotion at that time, I should have been blissful about what she was doing and put away my selfish unhappiness and began to value those little acts of affection. I should have been more responsive to her emotions and enjoyed its fruits. If I knew better, I would have fostered her emotions.

When Passion Mixes with Emotions

I asked that question to a couple who's been married for over twenty years. The husband replied by saying that he mixes his passion with his emotions. I asked what he meant by that. He said that he likes to say how nice his wife is when she wears a dress or tell her that she means everything to him and that he won't make it in this world if she's not there by his side. That's the way he expresses his emotion to his wife. In contrast, the wife likes to cuddle; she likes to hold his hands when they go out, and she likes to kiss him in spite of where they are. *"This is a good way of expressing my emotion,"* said the wife.

CHAPTER 6

Love and Emotions

NOT TOO LONG ago, I interviewed five men and five women about love and emotions. The question was, do men and women see emotions and love differently? The women articulated their views by saying that women love with their heart and mind, and men love with their mind and body. In contrast, the men were having difficulties explaining their views regarding this question. According to the women, some men do not know what love is. They explained that men think love is like loving chocolate ice cream, like loving a sports event or a car. If men understand the meaning of love, so will they understand why women are emotionally attached. Others may have different opinions.

After listening to the women and men, I began to ask the same question. Why are women so emotionally attached and men are not? Here are some answers:

1. To be emotionally attached is to make sacrifices, to love, to be committed, to forgive, to value, to empathize, to recognize, and to be compassionate.

2. Emotions are the single passion that gives life to our inner beauty.

3. To be emotionally attached is to have the breathtaking feeling of affection and kindheartedness toward a person.

4. To be emotionally attached is to experience the beauty and the power of love at the highest level.

5. To be emotionally attached is to trust one another and to create harmony.

6. To be emotionally attached brings excitement into lovers' lives. That is to say, lovers feel the butterfly emotions when they gaze into each other's eyes. Lovers who are emotionally attached are genuine and are able to lighten and to bring laughter to each other's heart.

7. To be emotionally attached means to obligate oneself with assurance, to give oneself completely to the

other person, and to form a strong bond, to flourish like roses in spring, to take risk, and to accept the cost of possible disenchantment.

8. To be emotionally attached is to assure oneself and your partner, and to freely express emotional thoughts without criticism.

9. To be emotionally attached is to allow the other person to discover your emotional quality. It means to share one's life, joys, and downfalls. Sharing takes strength and courage; sharing may keep a relationship strong.

10. To be emotionally attached is to learn to share one's past, present, and future with another person.

11. To be emotionally attached is to be kind and placid to one another.

12. To be emotionally attached is to be compassionate. Compassion is being able to care about the feelings and thoughts of another person. It is listening to and understanding one's needs and desires. Compassion means being definitely concerned about the health and well-being of another person.

13. To be emotionally attached is to practice the act of forgiveness. By human nature, every person is susceptible to making poor decisions, but the ability to forgive someone of his or her mistakes shows caring. Emotions are necessary components in a person's life. They are vital in every form to a friend, spouse, sibling, parent, or child. They add bliss and hope to a person's life. Emotions are powerful and beautiful if one knows how to demonstrate them.

14. Emotions play big parts in ways you love your partner. This is a love for your partner's inner beauty despite his or her emotional level. Emotions and love are usually accompanied by physical love. Physical attraction is one of the bases to form an emotional attachment.

CHAPTER 7

Attraction of a Man
Food like Oysters, Fish, and Passion Fruit
Attract a Man's Heart

COMPARED TO WOMEN, men are very weak. They need women in order to find their way in life. Not too long ago, a female friend said to me that a woman will get me if she knows how to cook. I tend to agree with her. I appreciate a woman's cooking. A woman who knows how to cook will get what she wants in a man.

Perfumes Attract a Man's Heart

My friend Joe said to me once that his girlfriend smells wonderful all the time. According to Joe, his girlfriend has the key to his heart because she always looks nice and clean. It is very true what Joe said. My male friends always told me that they love women who are clean and smell sensational.

Hairstyle, Sexy Dresses and Shoes Attract a Man's Heart

Flashy hair may not attract men, but good, clean, attractive hair may. Not too long ago, I was invited to a dinner party. I could not cease looking at a woman who was at the bar because of the way she fixed her hair, her sexy dress, her shoes. I had to get up and compliment her looks. Women, in order to get men, spend some time at the beauty shop, wear sexy dresses and shoes.

Is There a Planetary Difference between Men and Women?

Some books on gender differences take a dissimilar approach. It is very exciting to comprehend. The view that "men and women are from different planets" is not helpful scientifically. Both men and women have all the characteristics of a human being (hair, skin, blood, soul, and much more), but they tend to exhibit dissimilarity in the way they think. What makes them different? I think women are better listeners than men.

Being Good Listeners

Some researchers explain that emotion is about unexpected and logical changing into the other person's belief and feelings. It is not just about reacting to others' wrench or melancholy; it is about knowing the emotional ambiance between people. A man needs to be a good listener in order to be emotionally attached. A good listener can instantaneously sense when an emotional transformation occurred in someone, the cause, and what may make this particular person feel emotionally attached. Men need to be good listeners in order to respond naturally to a change in another person's feeling with apprehension, admiration, compassion, kindness, or whatever the apposite emotion might be.

A good listener shows compassion. Having compassion may lead you to stop at the flower shop and buy a bouquet of roses for your partner because you were thinking about her. For men to be emotionally attached, they need to be an innate listener and to be compassionate. A compassionate person can recognize when an individual is displeased with something or someone. A natural listener and compassionate person not only notices others' stance but also commonly thinks about what the other person is sensing, thinking of, or intending to do. They are emotionally attached when others are present or not.

What Does It Mean by Being Emotionally Attached?

Being emotionally attached ensures that you value a person, you notice others' feelings, and you fulfill one's necessities and desires. For example, a man may decide to love his woman no matter what.

Emotion in Relationships

Men and women value relations, but are there dissimilarities in what each gender values about other people? Women tend to value the growth of selfless, communal relationships. In contrast, men tend to value supremacy, politics, and rivalry

Communication and Emotion

One explains that women are more supportive, and more collaborative in communication than men. I agree with that thought. Emotionally attached women are primed to articulate what they feel and how they feel to others. When men note an offense, they are more likely to extract from it rather than working at repairing the relationship through tête-à-tête. From anger to sadness, from love to disgust, from delight to discontent, emotions flamboyantly affect our daily lives. So one could be asked, why do emotions have real impact in our lives? I believe emotion has a groundwork and consequence. Perhaps the emotions that are expressed by a wife may not have any direct effect on that wife, but her emotional reaction may affect the husband. Since emotions are typically needed to correspond successfully, this gives way to the possibility that emotions have real impact in our lives because they are the major funnel of our feelings.

The level of strength of our feeling relies on the amount of emotions we use. An emotionless person may not be able to express what he or she wants. Emotions precisely subsist to homogenize human being's self-confidence. Emotions may be used to praise and criticize someone. Emotions control a person's level of confidence and success.

Emotion Is a Very Powerful Skill

Many times men demonstrate their emotion by using words to display their comprehension, ability, and position. They are more likely to impress others. Women use their emotions to maintain personal and mutual relationships. A wife explains that she used her emotion to get what she wants from her husband. However, the husband showed his emotions by asking her to watch pornographic movies. People show their emotion in different ways.

Our emotions can affect our working ability. For example, employees at Disney World are trained on hospitality and are required to greet the customer with a smile, as well as cue and inform. As a nurse, I cannot let negative emotions affect my ability to provide excellent care to my patients.

Emotional Fitness

My father used to tell me that I need to eat well in order to be physically fit. However, he never told me how to be emotionally fit. I believe women are more emotionally fit than men are. I remember the story about two people who used to work in a similar job. Mark and Venetia were very close as coworkers. One day Mark told me that every time he saw Venetia, he wanted to hold her in his arms and kiss her. The question I asked Mark was, *"Do you have any emotional feeling for her?"* His response was, *"I guess so."* One day I called Mark and explained to him that he needed to let Venetia know how he felt about her. Finally he did what I asked him to do. Months later, their relationship was at the peak of their love.

Mark and Venetia became the ideal partners. Seven months later, Mark told me that he could not be in a relationship where a woman becomes insecure. My response was, *"Mark, I don't think Venetia is insecure."* Finally Mark explained to me by saying that he was afraid of showing his emotions to Venetia; therefore, he had to break up with her. After listening to his story, I realized that what Mark was experiencing was something that men experienced every day. Men are not emotionally fit to be with women who have the desires to show their emotions openly.

Men tend to hide their emotions when they are in a relationship. However, women tend to express their emotions in conversation without fear. Let's say a female visits another female. Both females may open a conversation like this: *"Oh, I love your shoes. You must tell me where you got them. They look so pretty on you. They really go well with your dress."*

Women talk about feelings and relationships when they converse to one another. In contrast, men talk about cars, jobs, and more.

The Flavor of Emotion

Emotions give our lives flavor, rejuvenate our inner beauty. Emotions help us to know how we feel about a person. Emotions give us the sense of being true to ourselves. Emotions boost our self-confidence. Emotions give us the ability to care, to cope, and to foster others despite the situation. Being emotionally attached is to forget one's self in order to value others.

How Do Both Genders Distinguish Emotions?

Women see emotions as men see emotions—as secure, insecure, attachment, estrangement, closeness, controlling, or threatening.

CHAPTER 8

Emotional Tips for Men and Women

MANY TIMES PEOPLE asked me how a man and a woman can show their emotion to each other. These tips may help if one tries them.

1. Express feelings openly to each other.

    Start by saying to one another how he or she feels. Do not hide anything from your partner. Offer your heart to your partner, not your mind. See your partner as your friend, not as a therapist. By doing so, it creates harmony and a strong bond.

2. Compliment each other's hair, dress, or clothes (tell him or her how nice and beautiful he or she is).

    Make remarks like *"Honey, your hair looks radiant. What did you do to your hair? I like it very much."* Do not criticize your partner's hair, clothes, or dress. Compliment should be every second, every minute, every hour. Compliment each other with a kiss.

3. Stop at his or her favorite store and buy him or her a gift.

    This shows how much you appreciate one another. It gives a sense of remembrance.

4. Place a bouquet of roses by each other's pillow and plant a good-morning kiss.

    This tip gives your partner the desire to feel complete and wanted. It is always necessary to combine your emotions with nature in order to fulfill each other's needs. It brings joy and delight. It rejuvenates the mind and the heart for love, and it strengthens emotions.

5. Snoop a beloved music as one or listen to each other's favorite music.

6. Have an intimate and cherished dinner.

7. Tell each other how much he or she means to you.

8. Go sailing together.

There is nothing more flamboyant than sailing together in a hot summer day. You two will have a splendid time.

9. Hold hands in public to strengthen the bond of love.

10. Men, carry your mate to her bed if able.

11. Let your lover live out his or her fantasies.

12. Take a passionate trip together.

13. Give to each other without expectation.

14. Be kind to your partner.

15. Whisper in each other's ear some love songs every day.

16. Talk face-to-face to each other.

17. Write a passionate memo to your partner, and post it for him or her.

18. Cook something together.

19. Feed one another in an intimate fashion to show your affection and your emotion.

20. Take the time to experience the savor of the food in your mouth and your partner's mouth.

21. Take a romantic picture together.

22. Say I love you by writing each other's name in a wall.

23. Flirt to one another.

24. Work as a team.

25. Be an encourager, not an advisor.

26. Visit a museum together.

27. Give back massage to one another.

28. Resolve conflict in a nonjudgmental fashion.

29. Pay attention to each other's need.

30. Discuss sex to one another.

31. Take a romantic bath together.

32. Support each other's emotion.

33. Value and respect one another.

34. Be fair to one another.

35. Do not engage in argument.

36. Collaborate to each other.

37. Have fun by having a romantic summertime activity or by going to a movie.

38. Go deep-sea fishing together.

39. Remember each other's birthday and anniversaries, and make it passionately special.

40. Spice up your sex life.

41. Do not be a pressure cooker, finally blowing up steam.

42. Don't stockpile issues. Solve them once they arrive.

43. Be loyal to one another.

44. Go out on a date.

45. Do not let the day go by without saying I love you.

46. Do not mock your partner for expressing himself or herself.

47. Do not undermine your partner's self-esteem.

48. Discuss with your partner what's in your mind.

49. Do not force your partner to do things that he or she does not want to do.

50. Do not control your partner's life.

51. Do not abuse your partner emotionally.

52. Be a friend, a lover, and a supporter to your partner.

Emotions are not deadly, and they are not diseases. No one should be afraid about expressing his or her emotions. Positively, emotions bring affection and spice up our daily attraction.

As one says, emotion is a *"passion."* It involves the body and the mind. Women are more emotionally attached than men. Many have discussed why women are more emotionally attached. It is because women are good *"empathizers,"* good listeners socially. Women act according to their intuition, and men act according to facts. Women talk about personal and intimate things. This demonstrates that women dissipate no time on uncongenial dialog but instantaneously move to tête-à-tête to the point where they can share their own feelings and intimacy.

Women's emotions are like roses that flourish in the spring season and like cold, icy lemonade in a hot summer day. As men, you don't have to be afraid when women display their emotions, you don't have to categorize them as being insecure. Women who are emotionally attached are like the rarest flowers found at the North Pole. Men need to explore and imitate that style in order to be emotionally attached. Men need to pay attention to the needs, not the problem.

Remedy for Emotions

Spend some time together to reflect on what's important for you and your partner by choosing a quiet and a suitable place. Don't fix on things which are not important. Choose a day that will be suitable for both of you to discuss finances and other issues regarding the relationship.

How to Get the Most out of Men

Start by being nice and by being a caring person toward your men. Being caring and nice bring a sense of closeness and a sense of belongingness to one another. Women, you need to be careful how you treat your men. Do not treat them as pet. When I talked to many women about how they get the most out of their men, they explained that they assessed themselves first. I asked them to clarify what they meant by assessing themselves. They used open-ended conversation with their men. For instance, instead of saying to your men that you want them to do something in a form of command, it is better to say it like this: would you like to do this? This style of questioning forms partnership, harmonizes both minds, and prevents internal conflicts.

Women need to know that men are dominant species. They want to be included as partners in any type of relationships. As dominant species, they will want to do whatever that is in their minds without seeing the consequences. However, they will express their sorrows later. Women are species of attraction and intuition.

As for men, they need to listen to their women when they express their feelings and their emotions. Men, don't be quick to compare your women with other women and vice versa. Both men and women need to respect one another.

www.ingramcontent.com/pod-product-compliance
Lightning Source LLC
Chambersburg PA
CBHW021304280526
45784CB00005B/2500